MUSICIANS INSTITUTE

PRIVATE LESSON

The Essential Guide to
Jazz Chord Voicings & Substitutions

by Scott Henderson

T0053157

Contents

ISBN 978-0-7935-9165-7

HAL•LEONARD®
CORPORATION
7777 W. BLUEMOUND RD. P.O. BOX 13819 MILWAUKEE, WI 53213

Visit Hal Leonard Online at
www.halleonard.com

Introduction

Hi. Thanks a lot for checking out this book. I think it will help you in your study of harmony and chord voicings on the guitar. With practice, this material can help you develop a more advanced harmonic vocabulary for accompaniment, composing, and chord-melody playing. I'll go into more detail about the voicings on the following pages, but first I would like to explain the reason I developed this system. It seems that whenever I see a chord manual, it's about an inch thick and filled with voicings that repeat many times throughout the book. Why? Because just about every chord can function as one or more other chords depending on which note is considered to be the root. So I decided to write a concise, easy-to-read chord book that clearly shows the possible uses of each voicing . . . and it's only sixteen pages long.

If you're wondering how to proceed through this book (it's short, but there's a lot to it!), first read through the opening pages; this material explains how I developed my chord system, how the voicings work, and some specific ways that you can apply them. Then, feel free to just start exploring the voicings.

Beyond that, here are a few suggestions:

- First, practice these voicings in the context of a tune or at least a chord progression. The ii–V–I progression would be a good place to start. Try to find voicings where the notes move smoothly (by a half or whole step) to the next voicing. For example, a Dmi7 with A on top, moving to G7(alt) with the A♭ on top, moving to a Cma7 with the G on top. Next, check out the inner voices of the chord and see if they are moving smoothly. There are many voicings in this book, and you'll find that some of them will move more smoothly than others depending on the context.

- Another very practical use for this book is to use it while composing or working on chord melody arrangements. When I'm composing, I use this system to change the roots under the voicing I've chosen to give me even more harmonic options.

- You should also experiment with the voicings on different string sets. I wrote some of the voicings using the first four strings and then again on the next four strings.

Last, but certainly not least, add your own voicings to this book. There are endless possibilities. Start with a chord in the book, change a note here or there, and many interesting things can happen.

Happy chording!

—Scott Henderson

Background Theory

First we'll need to cover some theory to clarify the concepts I used to develop this system. The voicings in this book combine chord tones with extended notes that embellish the basic underlying *chord types*—major, minor, dominant, minor7b5, diminished, etc. The extensions add color to the basic chord sound and are an important component in jazz improvisation, arranging, and composition. To illustrate the idea, let's start with a list of chord types, the intervals that make up the chords, and their available extended notes.

You can see from the table that each chord type has a number of available extensions that can be added to the basic chord sound. For example, the major chord type has three chord tones (root, 3rd, 5th) and four extensions (6, 7, 9, #11) for a total of seven notes that can be combined to create a "major" chord. Obviously, we can't play all these notes in one voicing on the guitar; however, we can play combinations of the chord tones and extensions, creating many different voicings, each with its own unique sound. Most of the voicings in this book will contain combinations of chord tones and extensions.

How the Voicings Work

Now that you are familiar with the chord types and the available extensions, we can look how my system works: Each chord type (listed on the top of each page) has a color. The colored numbers below each voicing correspond to the chord type colors. They are *not* fret numbers, nor do they have anything to do with positions on the neck. These numbers represent the interval of the **top note** of the chord, from the root of the chord type.

Let's look at this example:

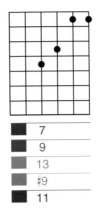

In my book, the color red represents major. The chord above can be used as a major chord since it has a red number. The red number 7 means that the top note of the chord is the major seventh. Let's be more specific: By playing this voicing at the 7th fret, making the top note a B natural, we get the following chords.

Cma7(♯11): The red number 7 indicates that the top note is the 7th of a major chord. If this top note is B, then the root of the chord is C. You could play the root with your thumb on the eighth fret.

Ami6/9: The blue 9 indicates that the top note is the 9th of a minor chord. If B is the 9th of the chord, the root is A. You could also include the root of this voicing by playing the open 5th string.

D13: The light blue 13 indicates that the top note is the 13th of a dominant seventh chord. If this 13th is B, the root of the chord is D. You could play the root with your thumb on the tenth fret.

A♭7(alt): The orange ♯9 indicates that the top note is the ♯9 of an altered dominant chord. If this ♯9 is B, the root of the chord is A♭. I use the first finger of my right hand to tap the A♭ (fourth fret on the low E string) to hear the chord as an A♭7(alt).

F♯mi7(♭5): The brown 11 indicates that the top note is the 11th of a minor 7(♭5) chord. If the 11th of the chord is B, then the root is F♯. Again, use your right hand to tap the root.

As you can see, there is *one* voicing here that can function as *five* different chords. By looking at the chord tones, extensions, and the intervals that make up the chords, we can learn more about the harmonic possibilities contained within a single voicing. When you apply this concept to each voicing, there are over 500 chords in this book! (As you work through the material, you'll notice that I left out the bass notes because they will change with each application of the chord.)

The previous example demonstrated how one voicing can be used to play several different chord types. Now let's look at another example to see how a single voicing can be used to create variations on one particular chord type. For this example, we'll look at a major chord.

By utilizing different extensions on the major chord type, the following voicing enables you to play three different chords within the C major tonality.

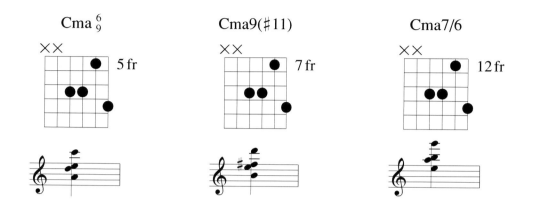

Melodic Minor

The main concept used in my system is based on the modes of the melodic minor scale. The scale is constructed by lowering the third degree of the major scale by one half step, resulting in intervals of 1–2–♭3–4–5–6–7. The examples below demonstrate how the scale can be used for improvisation over different chord types. These scales work well because they contain the chord tones and extensions suggested by the underlying chord.

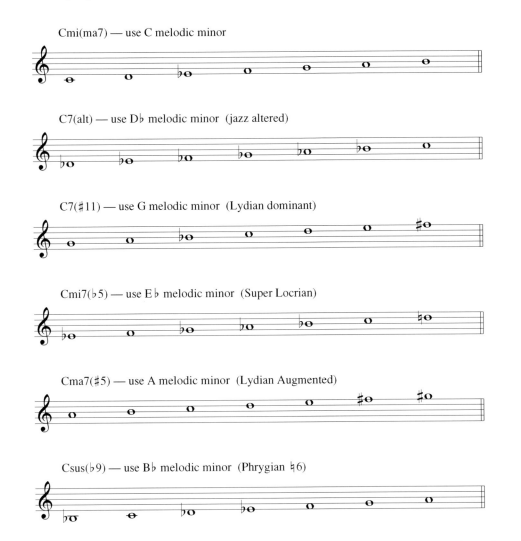

The same principle can also be applied to develop chord voicings from the modes of melodic minor.

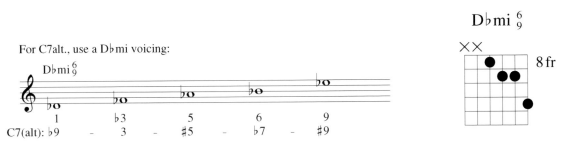

The D♭mi6/9 chord is derived from D♭ melodic minor by combining the 1–♭3–5 scale tones (D♭–F♭–A♭) with the 6th and 9th (B♭–E♭) extensions. Notice that the F♭ and B♭ in the chord imply the 3rd and ♭7th of the underlying C7 chord. The D♭mi6/9 includes the ♭9, #9, and #5 extensions of the C7 chord, creating a strong altered dominant sound.

Diminished Chords...

Now it's time to visit diminished land. Many people find this to be a confusing place, so I'll be as clear as I possibly can. The most common use of diminished chords in jazz is to play them a half step above the root of a dominant chord to create a Dom7(♭9) voicing. For example, by playing a D♭ diminished chord over C7 you have a C7(♭9) chord.

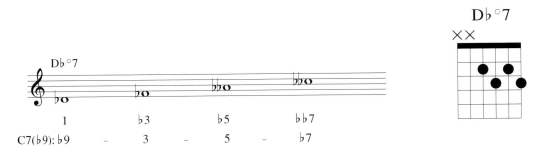

The other common application of diminished chords is to create connecting lines between diatonic chords as in the progression I–#I°–IImi. The symmetrical construction of diminished chords allows you to move them up and down in minor thirds creating different sounds while retaining the same harmonic function.

... and Symmetrical Altered Dominants

Like diminished chords, the altered dominant voicings in this book shown with an asterisk can be moved up and down in minor thirds to form three other altered dominant voicings. There are two families of these moving diminished/altered voicings, each with its own sound. The first group has the root of the Dom7th chord in the top note. If you move it in minor thirds you get the Root, #9, ♭5, and 13th extensions as the top note.

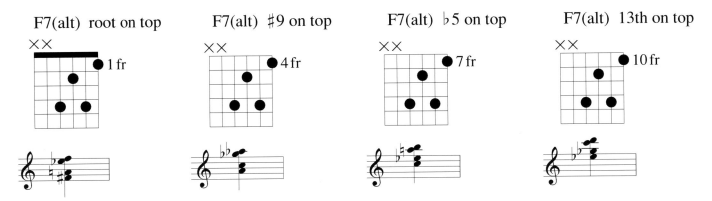

The second family of symmetrical altered dominant chords has the third of the dominant 7th chord in the top note. By moving it in minor thirds, you'll get the 5th, ♭7, and ♭9 on top; and although you have a different set of intervals in each chord, all of the voicings will function as altered dominants, each with its own sound.

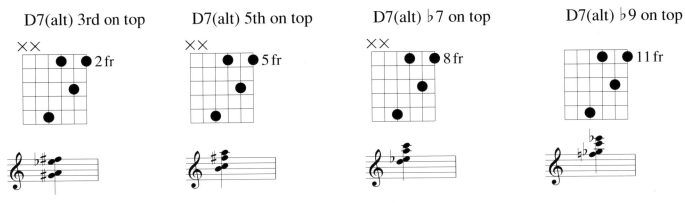

I didn't include all of these options for the symmetrical altered dominant chords within my system: the interval that I included is just my personal favorite of the four possibilities. Keep in mind that if a dominant 7th chord voicing does not contain a **natural 9 or a ♯5**, you can move it in minor thirds to create three more voicings which also function as altered dominant chords.

Of course, you may want to use these voicings as actual diminished chords instead of as altered dominants. In that case, the interval next to the altered dominant chord simply drops by a half step. For example, if you see an orange 3 next to an altered dominant voicing with an asterisk, that note functions as the ♭3 of a diminished chord. This voicing, for example, is a D♭ altered dominant, or a D diminished chord. Notice that the third of the altered dominant (F on the first string) becomes the ♭3 of the diminished chord. The diminished voicing utilizes the extension of the 9th (E) on the second string. Remember that the symmetrical construction of diminished chords allows you to move this voicing in minor thirds to form other diminished voicings.

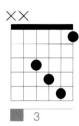

The Chords

| MA | mi | SUS | Dom7 | MA7(#5) | Dom7(alt) | dim | mi7(♭5) | mi(ma7) |

Row 1

| 3 / 5 / 9† | 3 / 5 / 9† | 5 9 / ♭7 / 4 | 5 9 / ♭7 / 4 | 7 / 9 / 6 |

Row 2

| 7 / 9 / 6 | #11 / 6 / 3† | #11 / 9 / 6 | 1 5 9 / ♭3 ♭7 / 4 / 3 | 1 5 6 9 / 1 ♭3 4 ♭7 / 1 4 ♭7 / ♭5 ♭9 |

Row 3

| 3 9 / 4 / 1 5 / #5 | 3 5 6 7 9 / 1 ♭3 4 5 ♭7 / 1 2 4 5 / #5 ♭9 #9 | 6 9 / 4 / 1 5† / #9 | 9 / 4 / 1† / #9 | 9 / 4 / 1† / #9 |

Row 4

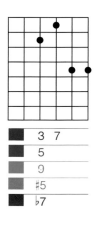 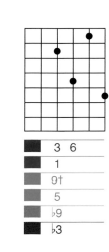 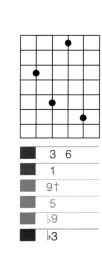 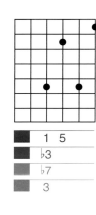 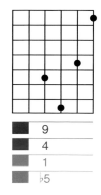 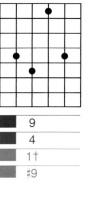

| 3 7 / 5 / 9 / #5 / ♭7 | 3 6 / 1 / 9† / 5 / ♭9 / ♭3 | 3 6 / 1 / 9† / 5 / ♭9 / ♭3 | 1 5 / ♭3 / ♭7 / 3 | 9 / 4 / 1 / ♭5 |

† = "suspended" chord with a major 3rd added.

* = Can be moved in minor thirds to create other altered dominant voicings.

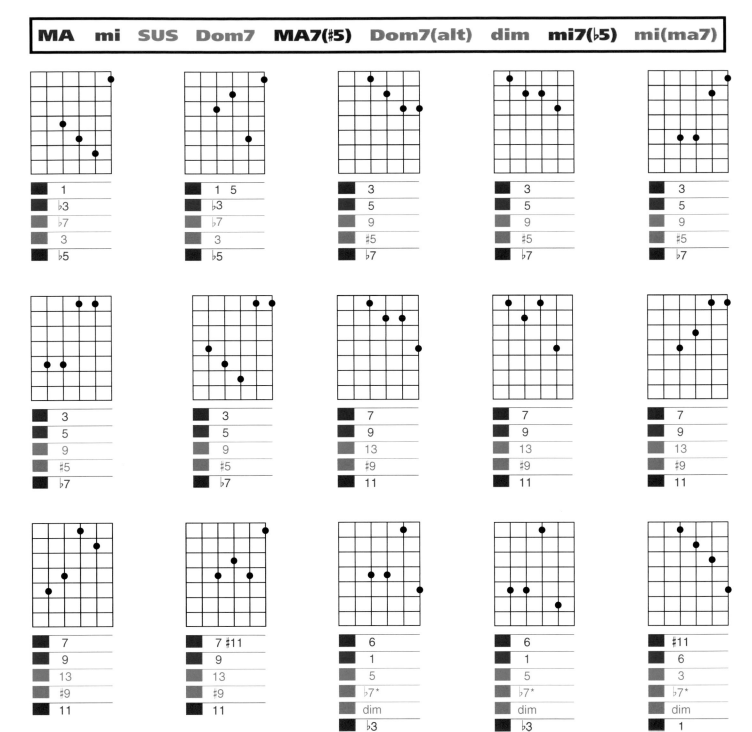
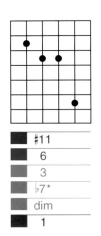
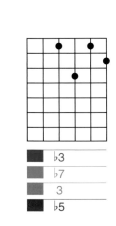
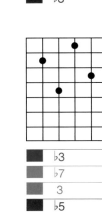
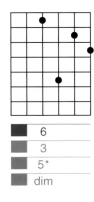
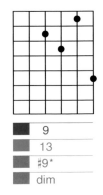

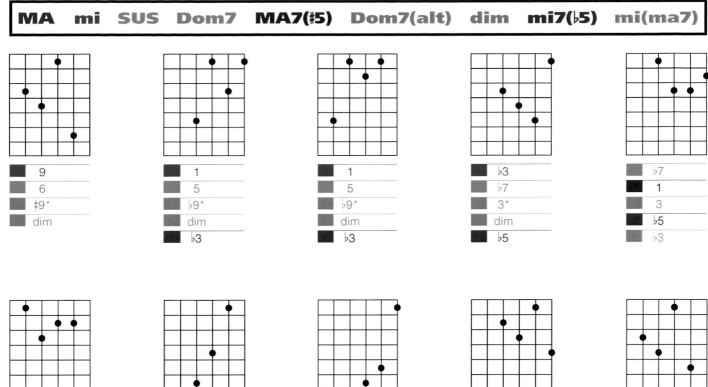

Row 1

9	1	1	♭3	♭7
6	5	5	♭7	1
#9*	♭9*	♭9*	3*	3
dim	dim	dim	dim	♭5
	♭3	♭3	♭5	♭3

Row 2

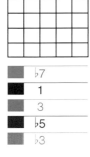
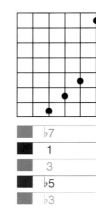
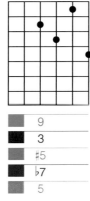
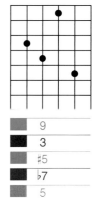

♭7	♭7	♭7	9	9
1	1	1	3	3
3	3	3	#5	#5
♭5	♭5	♭5	♭7	♭7
♭3	♭3	♭3	5	5

Row 3

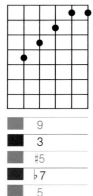

9	9	9	9	9
3	3	3	3	3
#5	#5	#5	#5	#5
♭7	♭7	♭7	♭7	♭7
5	5	5	5	5

Row 4

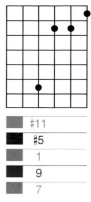

9	9	#11	#11	#11
3	3	#5	#5	#5
#5	#5	1	1	1
♭7	♭7	9	9	9
5	5	7	7	7

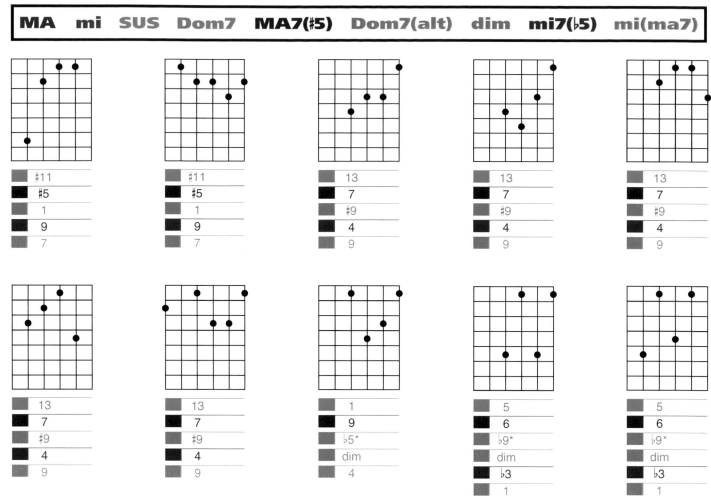

Row 1

#11	#11	13	13	13
#5	#5	7	7	7
1	1	#9	#9	#9
9	9	4	4	4
7	7	9	9	9

Row 2

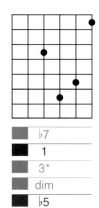  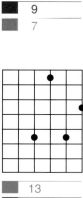 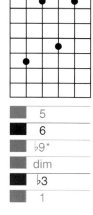 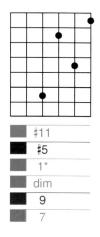

13	13	1	5	5
7	7	9	6	6
#9	#9	♭5*	♭9*	♭9*
4	4	dim	dim	dim
9	9	4	♭3	♭3
			1	1

Row 3

♭7	♭7	#11	#11	#11
1	1	#5	#5	#5
3*	3*	1*	1*	1*
dim	dim	dim	dim	dim
♭5	♭5	9	9	9
♭3	♭3	7	7	7

Row 4

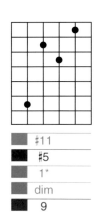 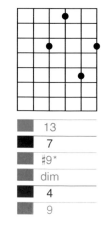 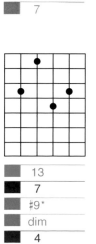  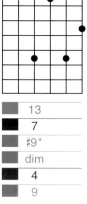 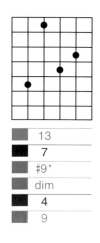

#11	13	13	13	13
#5	7	7	7	7
1*	#9*	#9*	#9*	#9*
dim	dim	dim	dim	dim
9	4	4	4	4
7	9	9	9	9

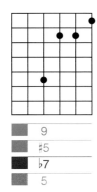
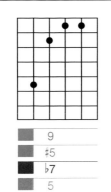
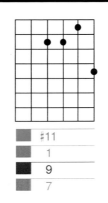
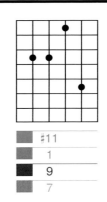
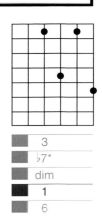

9	9	♯11	♯11	3
♯5	♯5	1	1	♭7*
♭7	♭7	9	9	dim
5	5	7	7	1
				6

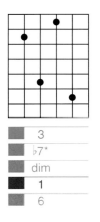
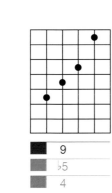
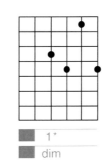
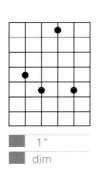
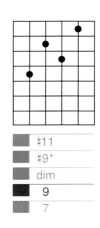

3	♭7	♭7	♯11	♯11
♭7*	3*	3*	♯9*	♯9*
dim	dim	dim	dim	dim
1	♭5	♭5	9	9
6	♭3	♭3	7	7

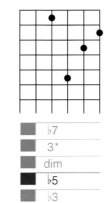
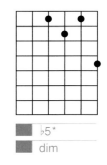

9	9	1*	1*	♭5*
♭5	♭5	dim	dim	dim
4	4			

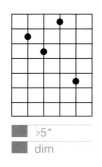
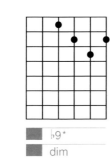
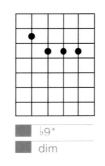
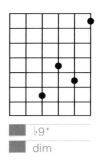
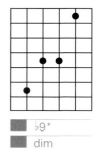

♭5*	♭9*	♭9*	♭9*	♭9*
dim	dim	dim	dim	dim

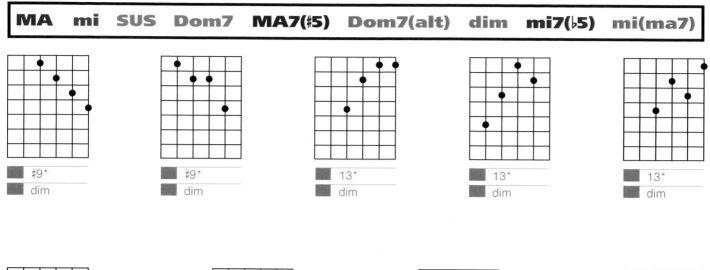

MA　mi　**SUS**　**Dom7**　**MA7(♯5)**　**Dom7(alt)**　**dim**　**mi7(♭5)**　**mi(ma7)**

| ■ | #9* |
| ■ | dim |

| ■ | #9* |
| ■ | dim |

| ■ | 13* |
| ■ | dim |

| ■ | 13* |
| ■ | dim |

| ■ | 13* |
| ■ | dim |

| ■ | 13* |
| ■ | dim |

| ■ | 13* |
| ■ | dim |

| ■ | 13* |
| ■ | dim |

| ■ | 13* |
| ■ | dim |